The 4 Ticcsters

A Family Of Tics & More

The 4 Ticcsters
A Family Of Tics & More

The Struggle of a Mother of Four Boys with
Tics, Tourette's Syndrome &
Obsessive-Compulsive-Disorder,
How You Can Learn From Our Experience.

Caris Poynter

The real moments and feelings were penned down to the best of the Author's ability, though the names were changed to protect the self-esteem of individuals.

Copyright © 2020 by Caris L. Poynter

Book design by Ali Iftikhar
Cover Photo by Robert Collins on Unsplash.com
ASIN: B088DCY5SR
ISBN: 9798644488391

For My Four Sons And Those Suffering From
Tourette's Syndrome & Obsessive-Compulsive-Disorder

I would like to thank **Ali Iftikhar,**
Who Put His Dedication And Hard Work Into
Editing Of This Book.

Special Thanks to The Facebook Support Group
Children With Tourette And Tic Disorders @CWTTD

Caris has always been a constructive person. She has mentored me and was there for me at the times of dismay. Her best quality is being passionate about understanding others. This book is exciting and written with pure emotions, to highlight the much-unanswered topic of Tics and Tourette. Her empathic nature has helped her kids fight the Tourette's, and her mission of spreading awareness is impressive. I ask everyone out there to read to this book if you are suffering from the symptoms or if you want to help others identifying the problem.

Penny Smith

Introduction

Getting the right diagnosis for your kids' mental health is the hardest part. If your Kids show Tics and you cannot get the correct diagnosis, you are in the same boat as I was. My children started showing Tics and indicators of other Disorders gradually. It was my Son Ramani, who was the first, not the eldest, who showed symptoms from the age of four, and it took me eight years to get the proper judgment. I was shattered and confused, not knowing what comes next, worried about the health of my children, overcoming my Bipolar and OCD. It was too much for me as a mother.

I researched and studied for the sake of my kids. I achieved the Level 4 Diploma for Counselling and Certification of Training in Mentoring. I wanted to make a difference by helping others with Addiction. Therefore, I wrote this book with a passion for reaching out to everyone with similar problems.

It is my humble effort to raise awareness of Mental Disorders. Identification of the symptoms is the first age, ready for my story, and you will come to know about the effort it takes to figure out the problem finally. I have developed ways of my methods from research, action plan from experience to fight it out. Only then can we overcome those. Ignoring the signs in your loved ones will bring you no good; it is time to face it!

The Four Boys Tic Path that you are about to read is based on my experience and life's journey. I have shared specific events and the feelings related to those moments to explain the difficulty. If you equip yourself with the suggestions provided, you will likely loosen up your shoulders and focus on what is required out of you. Take action, Intervene early, Know my story!

Caris Poynter

The 4 Ticcsters –

A family's of Tics and more

So now, I am aware that the sudden loud screeching noise from my son Ramani is another vocal tic. All this time, I thought it was him being silly or due to his hyperactivity because of ADHD. When we are sitting together, he is explaining himself to me, but he keeps having the urge to screech. This itch made me realise that this is what it was all along; an involuntary vocal sound called a tic!

We are still both learning collectively with new symptoms that appear suddenly, and I'm always making my son feel free. My son must be comfortable to speak to me about anything new or anything bothering him.

We both have similar characteristics, and he is aware of my motor tics. Imagine having to watch him at a young age exhibiting many motor tics such as involuntary eye-rolling movements. It was severe to the point where I thought it was a seizure, I had to take him to our local GP, and they referred us to a specialist in child development to find the cause.

When Ramani would become distressed and anxious, I would start finding papers with lists. He would need the list of football players' names, cars, family members, and mostly there would be numbers; since my kid is great at numbers and math. At the age of four, he would write all numeric 1 to 100 on a paper without my guidance. Even today, whenever he starts making lists, it is the early sign for me that he is anxious or something is going on.

This subject of Tourette's and OCD is very dear to me. I will go from each step of how it all happens in a family. The indications were all beginning; getting the diagnosis, and the battle with doctors is where I got pushed to the limits. I am very eager when it comes to this.

I write this from the heart and with passion as I go along. My son and I both suffer from OCD, and I would like to express the challenges we both glided through together and how far we have got. I have always wanted to get our story out there and make people aware that Tourette isn't just about swearing. It is so much more!

The worst tics for Ramani were in school. Moreover, teachers didn't understand he has a disorder called Coprographia, which is unintentional vulgar writings or drawings. Ramani would involuntarily use bad language words and draw sexual images on schoolwork, school tables, and even on his arms and hands. Without knowing this condition, it would look like this trait is deliberate, for attention.

However, for Ramani, it's embarrassing, and yet he doesn't have control. The feeling for him is intense, the same as motor tics when you are trying not to let it happen. It is almost impossible for a child with TS to stop his spasms at will.

Ramani would also repeat the sounds he heard or repeat other words that were said. People asked him questions, and Ramani had no control over his response and would be rude or offensive. This aggression would put him in a lot of trouble if people didn't understand he has Tourette syndrome. [1]

---

[1] (n.d.). Coprographia - Wikipedia. Retrieved May 7, 2020, from

Friends and family, who knew Ramani well, will always find his comments and tics funny and laugh it off. They will not degrade the poor boy; thus, it creates a peaceful arena for the kid. This comfort zone helps Ramani to be around the people close to him to feel relaxed and be himself. However, his reputation at school with many pupils unsettles him. Although he covers it up and disguises his tics very well, this makes it uncomfortable for the young lad. Considering, it brings more risk of having more convulsions appearing because he doesn't want people to know he has Tourette's or OCD.

Ramani's paranoia is a big deal, and he can't leave the house by himself. He has a belief that someone outside is going to put him in harm's way or, to very extreme, murder him. If he's out, he will always have to watch his back. If he sees anyone approaching him, Ramani would walk a different way or run towards the opposite side. He would start shaking, sweating, and feel endangered. This reaction would also make the tics worsen because stress, anxiety, and many other emotions make tics appear.

While playing computer games online with friends, Ramani would tic more, and the vocals would become apparent. He would shout the word 'nigger' or speak sentences related to paedophilia such as 'I touch kids' or say "shut up, or I'll touch you." He would also come out with "if she's old enough to bleed, she is old enough to breed"! Yeah, this isn't precisely something others will appreciate hearing in public or over gaming. However, remember, these are involuntary vocal tics, and Ramani has no control of what he had said.

Furthermore, Ramani would make sexual gestures. This one day, as we're heading to our next London doctor's appointment, Ramani had an extremely hyperactive mood, and being in crowded places makes tics worsen. While we are standing up on the underground train and the tube is full of people. Ramani would start grinding sexually against the pole he's holding onto, saying sexual words, and he was unable to stop. These are common tics with people who have Tourette to make gestures, including putting the middle or two fingers up. He would also perform other sexual gestures.

As a mother who knows her son, I could only laugh along with his brother, who is one year younger, because what else could we do? I recognise he can't help this Behaviour. So many people were staring at us. I was embarrassed, and so was his brother. Still, we took it in a light mood only because we knew Ramani and his character.

We had a fall out with Ramani's paternal side of the family, who got to watch one video I sent to Ramani's stepmother for support. She showed someone else, and that person didn't know Ramani at all. The video was of Ramani speaking strange words and sentences. This tape made the other family believe Ramani is a paedophile! He's 13 years old for god sake, it's impossible. I tried to fight back and tell them it's Tourette's automatic Behaviour; my son can't help it.

Conversely, they didn't believe me and sent offensive messages to me saying my son's a monster. I should tell the police he is a danger to the kids. If only they had researched and understood what the condition was and spent time with Ramani so they would be able to support him, but they didn't want to.

Ramani's tics can disappear for a while but then come back to a significant extent. His explanation of how a twitch feels like being a sensation you get if you open your eyes and can't blink. At that time, you start to feel uncomfortable, pain in the eyes, and all you think about is to flick the eye.

The intense feeling and urge you have are unbearable that before you know it, you have blinked. That satisfaction afterwards is a relief and a good sense inside that you did it because you were uncomfortable if you didn't.

Although only Ramani has the diagnosis of Tourette Syndrome, I start to wonder if there is any misunderstanding with my other boys with Tics. Doctors have declared their condition as a Tic disorder when, in fact, they might have TS too!

1st Chapter: My Journey

During childhood, I had seen many things as a child that I shouldn't have. I also had my younger sister, growing up together, who is three years younger than I am. My mum was disabled; she had Muscular Dystrophy and a mental health condition called Bipolar.

My biological father had left when I was a baby. I never had much contact with him. He would only turn up once a year just because he was nearby. He wouldn't stop long and spent most of the visiting time speaking to my mum. The only thing I knew about my real dad was he's a big-time gambler and was in prison at some point. Around the age of 6, my mum married my stepdad; I always called him by his name Jim. He had health problems of his own, including Epilepsy.

My sister and I were close, and I could always rely on her looking out for me if ever I was in trouble. She was more of a tomboy and had very challenging Behaviour. My relationship with my mum isn't evident from what I remember but wasn't an emotional connection. I never told her I loved her or held her hand or kissed her cheek as children do, and I don't remember her giving me any love. My stepdad and I also had a similar relationship; I just couldn't feel close to any of them. I still don't know to this day why.

I do remember my mum having other men in and out of the house; also, she would often argue with my stepdad. On one occasion, I witnessed him having an epileptic fit on the floor; this is a scary experience for any young child to see!

Once Jim was admitted in a mental hospital because he became suicidal and threatened to jump from the multi-storey car park. Hearing this as a child is very hurtful, and I didn't know how to deal with my feelings and had no one really to explain anything to me. My sister would also witness this with me, but we never spoke about it together.

When I got to the age of 10, my mother had given birth to my brother Ben. Unfortunately, he had the same disability as my mum. He was monitored in the hospital for six months from delivery on ventilators. Although the docs told us he wouldn't survive to the age of 1, Ben proved them wrong and reached the age of 12. He sadly passed away with pneumonia. Ben was put in foster care from the age of four, because my mum's condition deteriorated, and she couldn't look after him any longer.

Living in a small bungalow when Ben was born, we had a close family member move in with us called Bob. Not long after the guy moved in, Social Services contacted my mum and Jim. There was a concern for the welfare of myself and my sister being around the alleged convict! Apparently, in their records, Bob was a Convicted Paedophile. The officers told my parents that the supposed offender had to leave the premises, or they will have to take my sister and me into protection.

Well, Bob was still living with us. One month later, the social service puts my baby sister and me on the Protection Register list. We were also assigned a social worker to visit often and question us both about the home life and if he had touched us or if he's still living with us.

We were told to lie and say Bob had left, but he hadn't.

Bob was also my mum's driver as she was disabled, and the only one whom she knew could drive, so he would often take us to school and back. Besides, Charmaine and I would be alone with Bob in the home, at times. The one thing we never understood was, he never once touched us sexually or inappropriately! Consequently, my parents questioned the social workers' accusations, and Bob denied being convicted and affecting children improperly. Even now, I can say that not once the so-called molester touched us as a child, we sisters had spoken about this often. As adults, to this day, we are confident we were never touched inappropriately by the alleged felon. We would question ourselves if he were a Paedophile.

My sister Charmaine was a challenging child, demanding, oppositional, and controlling. My mum was even scared of her to some extent. Charmaine mixed with the wrong crowd of people and ended up becoming a drug and alcohol addict. The Addiction led her to snip from family and rob off strangers in their homes. She even stole from me many times.

I remember when Charmaine was around the age of 11; my Nan said to my mum that, "Charmaine's going to end up on drugs and in prison," she was right! Charmaine also bullied me, pressured me to do what she wanted, and even threatened me if I didn't meet her demands. Not only she did this with me, but also she will do the same for adults, including my mum, Jim, and our uncle George.

Charmaine's Behaviour was never understandable; she never was satisfied with anything, was often aggressive, and had tantrums no matter where she was. She never cared who would be standing there, staring at her in shock and disgust. She would even get in fights with men and women.

Years later, in early adulthood, Charmaine ended up in prison for a year for fraud and was released on the tag to live with me for three months. Charmaine always had me to fall back on, and I never judged her, or I could never turn my back on her. Many people don't believe she's even my sister because we are different characters, but brought up together in the same way!

I'm known as the soft one, maybe I look easy to some people, and I was shy in school. I am just too thoughtful of others and always have been an emotional person. If I see someone crying, I will cry. I'm empathetic.

At the age of 15, I quit school. After all, I wasn't going to succeed and pass my GCSE's because I had not attended my classes enough! The school was a complicated part of my life, as well as being at home. I was bullied for almost anything possible for the bullies to look macho to their friends. I had fallen behind so much in my academic work; it was not possible to catch up.

Every morning Jim would wake me up to get ready for the school. Instantly I'd feel anxious, and I would find ways of skipping. Every day, excuse after excuse, faking being sick to leave the house and staying on the streets until school ended. I still don't know, to this day, exactly what my feelings towards school were and what caused the anxiety so bad to make it very difficult to leave the house. I'd cry and cry so much, begging my mum not to let me go to school. I would do anything to stay at home.

The bullying wasn't the leading problem, but it didn't help, but what else was giving me this strange sense and fear to not go to school. I just could never explain or understand myself. Some days I would be OK and happy to go to school, but 90 per cent of the time, it was very hard for me.

At 16, I started my first relationship and fell pregnant with my first child, Rye. I also left home and got myself a small flat with help from an association and a social worker.

After experiencing so much in life, I finally found my partner, a healthy and stable relationship. Sonny changed me so much. He showed me what love is and how real it can be. Before Sonny comes along, I was empty, alone, lost, and confused as to whom I was and what I wanted in my life. Then Sonny came into my life and made me smile again; he gives me a feeling inside I never knew existed! Feelings I am scared and afraid to think because I do not want this feeling to end. He shows me just how much love he has for me. It is incredible, and the most amazing and unique love I have NEVER had before! I am head over heels with him (infatuated). Every day I long to (really want) to touch him and kiss his lips softly with all the passion I have inside me and the happiness that he makes me feel. I adore Sonny! He has given me strength and power. How I feel for him is something that words cannot describe. When he kisses me, I have a happy tear in my eye and a strong, powerful feeling in my body, and this is what love does!

Sonny has lightened up my life, given me so much hope, and taught me how to become a better person. I am who I am because of him!

When I am with Sonny, I feel safe and secure. My boys and I trust him to protect my family and me, and I trust that he will not let anything or no one destroy what we have! This love and family that we have together is unbreakable. I believe in us, and I have faith that we will make it to the end Together! I will love him for as long as the stars are in the sky and more. I crave his attention and his touch, I am addicted to him, and I'll always thank him for standing by me when days are grey.

I have overcome and seen so much in life; it only made me an improved person. I completed my **Diploma in Counselling** and a **Certificate of Training in Mentoring**. I had my experience with my sister being an addict, and thought I would use my knowledge to help others.

2nd Chapter: Tourette Syndrome & OCD

Did you ever observe a child shrugging without knowing, blinking unadvisedly, or divulging visceral churlish reaction? That sudden utter of sounds, bursting out with hostile words, and flickering the eyes are symptoms of a neurological disorder. Who would have thought, this is not an ill-mannered kid, and the poor soul is suffering from a Medical Condition? That could be Tourette syndrome (Pronounced as too-Ret), and one should not judge a child by his Behaviour so quickly.

At the age of two to fifteen years[2] is when the indications are visible in a child suffering from the syndrome. The average age of early signs of TS is six years, the same as my dear Kodie. These signs are known as Tics, and it could be unusual words, eye-rolling, little movement of shoulders, lip twitching, or inappropriate sounds. It is important to note here that men are more vulnerable to develop these inconsiderate reactions than women are. Hence, my handsome four boys are prone to this despicable syndrome. One could make strange voices without even a thought, and this is often embarrassing for the person suffering, as people start bullying the victim.

You must have seen a tic here and there, even if you are not a parent, without knowing. The kid in the supermarket, for instance, with a sudden shrug which looked a bit out of shape. The youngster with a lot of blinking, in a theme park, ever caught your eye? We all have come across a young chap with single or multiple tics without realisation. It is altogether familiar, and there is no high risk involved in every tic because not every spasm is dangerous. As a parent, when you find out your child has developed a twitch, it is always best to visit your paediatrician and confirm it. If the doctors confirm the presence of Tics, only then the possibility of timely intervention sees the light of day.

The Tourette's is not curable as of now. Still, I hope that somebody soon finds a cure for it so that my angels and the many suffering from it could live an ordinary life. Nevertheless, there are treatments and therapies in place, and people take benefits from those. Although the therapy sessions help one suffering from TS, most people discourage it by saying that it will go away with age. My question is, why.

---

[2] (2018, August 8). Tourette syndrome - Mayo Clinic. Retrieved May 5, 2020, from https://www.mayoclinic.org/diseases-conditions/tourette-syndrome/symptoms-causes/syc-20350465

Would you let your sweet child just suffer from it until it finally decides to go away after the teenage years? Not! I will fight it, for the sake of my kids, and manifolds of others undergoing the same. In a broad sense, my mission is to raise awareness among the parents who ignore such an uncontrolled prodromal stage in their children. No parent would tolerate their next of kin in distress of unwanted moves, or to blurt out abusive words. No one should!

My kids are all boys. The early stages of Tourette in their lives played a role of catalyst in my life. Because I was continually observing the signs, and I could feel there is something wrong, I started researching and studying on my own. People always told me that I worry too much, but I was never able to get a diagnosis out of a shrink. I had to battle my way through, and finally, the experts declared it as a Tourette syndrome. You can't fight an enemy you can't identify. It is so important to realise what you are up against, to overcome it.

My memoir intends to inspire other parents not to ignore the worrying signs and address it like an adult. TS is like the elephant in the room, everyone can see it, but nobody wants to talk about it. It is crucial to discuss it, to debate the issue and come up with a solution. I know that a young person eventually learns to control these Tics if the spasms don't diminish by themselves. But imagine the years of discomfort for the little soul, who has gone through so much early in life. Just picture a child, with involuntary motor trembling or vocal jerks, having to face the cruel world full of bullies.

Tourette's syndrome is quite common among adolescents, and it needs to differentiate from a Tic disorder, which is the primary cause of TS. A patient of Tic disorder[3] would need edifying reflection and alert waiting with watchful eyes. One's parents need to be vigilant towards unusual habits or sudden bursts of anger in their children because early intervention is the only way out. If the young person of your family is flickering his/her eyes or having weird quivers, it is time to consult the paediatrician. You could avoid the palpitation from worsening by nipping the tic in the bud.

---

[3] (n.d.). Tic disorder - Wikipedia. Retrieved May 5, 2020, from **https://en.wikipedia.org/wiki/Tic_disorder**

What is Tourette's syndrome? Let's talk in medical terms first, and later conclude a definition in layman's terms. The worrying tics are the synchronised different types of movements/actions, described as mainly Motor, Phonic, and also based on the duration.[4] These actions, though all involuntarily, could be swift, without rhythm, or recurring. The severe outcome of these tics is Tourette syndrome, a disorder needing medical attention.

We can define TS as a compilation of a variety of motor tics and no less than a singular phonic spasm. When the symptoms transform into Tourettism with severed movements, fears, and genetic history, simply put, it is Tourette's syndrome. These disruptive behaviours can be co-morbid with a plethora of other neuropsychological conditions. Still, they can go unnoticed by half-hearted observers. Therefore, a parent is the best judge to identify the symptoms, consult with the doctors, and come up with an outcome.[5]

If only recently, you see your child showing a tic, there is good news and bad news. The good news is, nearly all tics fly-by on their own, and there is no dire need for treatment. You could simply wait it out. If the spasms are chronic, then this is a piece of bad news. The lion's share of seizures fades away unattended; however, if those tweaks stick around for more than a year, it could be Tourette's.[6]

Compulsions, monotonous routines, maddening desires are all the signs of OCD (Obsessive Compulsive Disorder). One out of hundred

---

[4] (n.d.). Diagnostic criteria for 307.23 Tourette's Disorder - Behavenet. Retrieved May 5, 2020, from **https://behavenet.com/diagnostic-criteria-30723-tourettes-disorder**

[5] (n.d.). Tourettism - Wikipedia. Retrieved May 5, 2020, from **https://en.wikipedia.org/wiki/Tourettism**

[6] (n.d.). Tics and Tourette's | Child Mind Institute. Retrieved May 5, 2020, from **https://childmind.org/article/tics-and-tourettes/**

Americans has OCD, the anxiety complaint of habitual actions, or cyclical thoughts. The criteria for diagnostics are the recurring thought process or compulsions, which are visible in a patient for over twelve months. The condition often begins in the early stages of life.[7]

There are numerous types of Obsessions which are under the classification of OCD. These obsessions include Sexual thoughts and fear. Other forms related to extremism are Perfectionism and Religious extremism. Fear is a broad term, and it could relate to a fear of losing control or catching a disease. These obsessions can appear in a healthy person's mind, but an OCD patient has severe effects on his daily life.[8]

OCD's symptoms can appear similar to those of ADHD, Autism, and other disorders. A person with OCD could be washing his hands without any need because, in his mind, he feels contaminated. He could be obsessed about closed doors and orders and resultantly will keep on re-checking. It is crucial to recognise the anxiety triggers and learn how to avoid those situations. The patient who has Obsessive Compulsive Disorder will develop unwanted obsessive thoughts and, consequently, anxiety. He will feel the need to act upon his obsession to feel relaxed. The nervousness will lure the person into compulsive Behaviour. [9]

Although Obsessions are unwelcome notions, Compulsions are the actions provoked by obsessive feelings. One would try to fight a compulsive behaviour knowing it is wrong, but the neurotic force will overcome him. A compulsion is the reaction or aftermath of

[7] (n.d.). What Is Obsessive-Compulsive Disorder?. Retrieved May 7, 2020, from https://www.psychiatry.org/patients-families/ocd/what-is-obsessive-compulsive-disorder

[8] (n.d.). What is OCD? - International OCD Foundation. Retrieved May 7, 2020, from https://iocdf.org/about-ocd/

[9] (2020, April 15). Obsessive-Compulsive Disorder (OCD .... Retrieved May 7, 2020, from https://www.helpguide.org/articles/anxiety/obssessive-compulsive-disorder-ocd.htm

obsessive thoughts. It is so strong that it becomes an addiction, and the person keeps on repeating it. The idea of contaminating a loved one, for instance, will force you to wash your body parts again and again. [10]

[10] (2020, April 15). Obsessive-Compulsive Disorder (OCD .... Retrieved May 7, 2020, from https://www.helpguide.org/articles/anxiety/obssessive-compulsive-disorder-ocd.htm

3rd Chapter: OCD experiences of a mother and son

My therapist once told me that you could be addicted to anything such as drugs, alcohol, cigarettes, and unbelievably, sex!

In the past years, I have had many different obsessions/addictions that I didn't know how to control. I didn't realise I was addicted to certain things, including becoming obsessed with one hobby, then losing interest after a specific time. Formerly another different hobby comes along, and I waste myself obsessing over that.

When I had this primary Addiction at the time, I cannot stop thinking about the subject. For example, I suddenly had a high interest in baking cupcakes! I hate cooking, and I never thought I would become interested in baking cakes at all. I researched how to bake, what ingredients I needed, and appliances to be able to cook.

Every time I was searching on google, studying, or watching YouTube videos on baking cakes, I was sensing a high energetic feel like buzzing.

I couldn't stop thinking of what I want to do with this leisure pursuit. I was up until late at night, losing sleep with a constant obsession over baking cakes. Payday comes, and that was it, all my money went on what I needed to buy for baking. Moreover, I started to bake for a couple of weeks. I spent money on this interest without thinking of the consequences of having to pay bills etc.

I was feeling well and pleased when I had the adrenaline rush, but at the same time, if I didn't act on this urge to spend on this hobby and work on it, I'd feel agitated and restless. I had no control over how to stop the call! I was ADDICTED.

After a little while, maybe a month later, I lost all interest in baking at once! I had wasted time and extravagant money on something where I no longer had an affair. The high feeling, the buzz, and adrenaline, all had gone.

A new day comes, and again, another addiction/obsession comes along!
This time around, it's art and crafts, I'm not creative and never had interest ever before, but once again, this pattern is the same as "the baking habit." The great feel of a live buzzing and adrenaline is back to the arts and crafts, money wasted, along with the time. After all the vivacious spending, I am on the same crossroads again because, subsequently, the interest had gone away.

I've had other obsessions such as joining the gym, learning to play the piano, and the fascination with a guitar. At one time, I wanted to become a counsellor/mentor, and I even studied at home and passed the course of counselling. Yet again, after a time, I didn't want to grow into this anymore!

Items I've also obsessed about and had strong, intense urges to buy whatever it was I had to buy to keep the feeling inside to make me fulfilled. It's like a drug, something I obsess about was keeping me high and excited, and I had to act on this to keep the good-feeling intact.

I was even once addicted to dating sites! I was getting satisfaction from signing up and making profiles for searching people and messaging. I couldn't come off the applications, and I could not stop the urge to search the profiles and chats, this took over a lot of my time. I didn't fathom why this was happening. What was the reason for feeling good adrenaline over dating applications? This Addiction took a long time for me to stop and realise it was the most prolonged obsession I had. I still don't understand how this could have become an addiction.

Now, I somehow understand how people, who are gamblers, feel, and have no control over how to fight the impulse not to set foot in the bookies.

When you don't act on the compulsion towards the obsession, then you're going to feel awful, agitated, restless, angry, and feel you're going to lose your mind. It is all you think about; there is nothing else you want to do. It becomes impossible to concentrate on anything else other than wanting to go to the casino and gamble! It is not about whether you will win or not; it's the feeling of adrenaline.

The intense high feelings of happiness and excitement rise. You desire to walk through that door to place the bet and wait for the outcome. However, when you lose, of course, you are down; you lose money and are overwhelmed with the guilt! The same feeling I get when I don't act on anything I obsess over or addicted to that particular thing.

Paranoia becomes a problem for me and is an uncontrollable and disturbing thought I have that is intrusive. I know I won't act on this thought. Still, the feeling I get is intense and impossible to stop the idea and have to avoid doing things to stop being scared.

Standing at the train station waiting for my train to arrive and I locate it ahead of its arrival. My mind instantly pictures myself, jumping in front of this train. I'm confused and terrified of this thought and scared, but also distressed because I know I won't act on this. I'm afraid to look at the train coming towards me, so I look away until it stops!

I have developed a fear of sleeping because if I do, I envision in my mind that someone is intruding on my home, to go upstairs to my bedroom and attack me. The longest my eyes are closed, the more my mental version of someone getting closer and closer to me will strengthen. Once I open my eyes, this vision is gone, and I'm safe.

I have a son aged 14. Ramani. He also is suffering from OCD and paranoia. Consequently, his feelings are not controlled by his thoughts to do actions he had never done before. At a young age, at around 4years old, he would ask for help to put his shoes on. I'd attend and grab the right footwear to put on for him, and in a sudden moment, he would scream, beg and beg for me to put the left shoe on first, I never understood why. I'd ask why and what's wrong and ask him to calm down because he was extraordinarily agitated and stressed, but once I changed the right shoe from the left, his response stopped and was calm. I could see the change in how relaxed he was.

This episode went on for months, and I thought at first that he was just trying to control me. I assumed he wanted to get attention when, in fact, he didn't have any control over himself for this reaction. It was a warning sign from his OCD that took me a while to realise. After maybe one year, this shoe problem of having to be left put on first stopped, but then comes another pattern, and that thought in his mind for a second time took over, not just him but lured me in too. Nighttime has always been a bedtime story, we sit together in my son's bed, and I'd open the first page and start to read aloud to him. A few pages in, I would continue to narrate the story for my son to become very aggressive suddenly. He would ask me to recite that sentence again because it's wrong, I re-read the line in the same tone I did before. Still, with aggression and crying, he begs me to repeat and says it's wrong how I said it. After having this problem many times, ultimately, I narrated the sentence in a way that calmed him down and made him relax so that I could continue the book.

It wasn't until after a lot of researching and seeing his doctors that I pieced together this was typical OCD behaviour. This condition would force him to feel uncomfortable if I didn't say the sentence in a specific tone. To feel safe, he would push me to re-read it for him. Never did I think this would be an OCD problem, but it was. We always felt complicated at the time of the bedtime stories; it was tough for us.

The more I did not deliver the story pitched in the right tone of the sentence, I had read to my son previously, the most intense pain and fear he felt. When it was all in vain, I had to bury myself in. I could do nothing more than to feed upon what he wanted me to say for as many times until it felt just right to him!

After some time, this OCD pattern with my son vanished, but another appeared. Once I tuck my son to bed and kissed him good-night, I would walk away, but then he would suddenly shout to me to touch the top of his duvet! Now bear in mind at this time, I thought OCD was about cleaning hands or things in order. When I'm having all these orders from a 4 to 5-year-old, this seems like he wants to gain control over me, to perform everything he wants. If I don't do it, he will go crazy!

To keep him from being angry and crying after refusing to do what he ordered me, I'd make sure of what he wanted, so I'd turn back towards him in the bed. I would fix what he had instructed, and that is to tap the top of his duvet. Would you believe just by meeting this demand, he stopped crying and being angry suddenly, and he was able to lie down and relax.

Can you see that there's a pattern of not just my son being distressed, but I am too? Because I didn't know what this was all about and other people suggested he's trying to control me, but as a mum, I had something telling me it's something more, but what?

I'll never forget the time my son would arrive in the evenings after being with his dad the weekend from Friday to Sunday. At around 7 pm Sunday evenings every week, my son would come back home in his dad's car. They would park straight in front of the front door.

I'd hear the car arrive, and I'd open my house front door before my son got out of the vehicle. Well, this started to become a problem for my son because he wanted to knock on the door before I opened it! Why? I asked him, and my son couldn't explain the reason, but again became annoyed. He started hitting me, shouting, crying, and begging me to shut the front door and let him knock first. At this time, I refused to feel controlled and said, "no." But there was no calming my child at all. He was going red in the face, shaking, and very agitated. What else can I do but now let him take control? I closed the door and let him knock first, and then I could open the door afterwards. Can you see the power this OCD had, was not just after my son, but now I'm involved and consumed by it?

Either way, I had no choice but to redo the task every time, by closing the door and letting him knock for me to then open again. Instantly he would be calm and able to walk into the home! Yet I am shocked how quickly just completing that demand would make him change so fast and transformed.

Now by my own experience, understanding, and thorough research of many years, I had established a little knowledge of OCD. Still, this Behaviour from my son and me wasn't what I expected, and I had learnt that this was OCD.

Firstly, we see the pattern and our compulsion to act upon what we feel at the time and what our thoughts are telling us. Moreover, we have little or no control over this sensation, and no one can understand what was going on inside our minds. Nonetheless, nobody knows nor understands the emotional state we have. The intense anger, rage inside ourselves was overwhelming our attention. Nothing could distract us from other things. We end up having no choice but to act upon this craving. We ultimately perform the compulsive gait to feel safe, secure, and comfortable within ourselves.

4th Chapter: Tics and More!

From the age of three to the age of seven, my son had developed both vocal and motor tics lasting years at intervals of waxing and waning, etc. These grunting, sniffing, saying inappropriate words, eye-rolling, and additional movement tics, made me fully aware after my research that this was a criterion of Tourette's syndrome.

It is essential to identify different types of Tics so that if your kid starts developing a tic, you would be able to recognise it. I want you to be able to make a decision and to go out and take action as early as possible. Please do not ignore the Tics, if any, in your children and intervene as quickly as possible. You don't want to spend eight years like me, just to get the diagnosis. It can change your kids' lives and yours with them.

A tic is the small movement of limited parts of a person's body without control. What happens is: your brain sends a signal to that muscle to move in a certain way when there is a trigger. The trigger could be anxiety, pressure situation, or anger. You might start shrugging your shoulders, shouting out words, nodding your head, or begin moving your eyes without realisation. Experts categorise tics on a broader level in two groups, Simple or Complex. Simple twitches are the repetition of grunts, sniffs, throat-clearing sounds, snorting, barking mimicking, coughs, or hand movements. [11]

In contrast, the Complex tics involve grimacing your face, shrugs, nods, twisting the head, touching an object, and even punching or severe vocal spasms. In this scenario, one can start uttering words or phrases that are morally incorrect, abusing, for example. This symptom classifies as Coprolalia, possibly, where you start calling other names or blurt-out swears of your own. All of these moves are without intention; although they might look decisive, they are not.[12]

When we watch a TS patient in movies or TV serials, it is all about swearing. Whereas, in reality, it is only 10-15% of Tourette's patients that utter abusive or immoral words. It is essential to understand that the syndrome's patient has an uncontrollable itch just to end it. They feel a powerful sensation to perform the tic for a certain period or in a particular way to satisfy the thirst. These twitches are present while asleep but mostly at a minimal level. The repetition, speed, intensity, and body parts could always vary from time to time. TS starts mainly with the upper body part and can transfer to any body part once severe.[13]

Vocal and Motor tics could be either complex or simple. Vocal twitches are phonic and could range from words to sentences. Adversely, Motor tics are related to movements of body parts and develop at the later stage than Vocal twitches. Patients can disguise a few tics, suppress others, or can't help themselves with some. Although not every Tic is Tourette's, if they last for about a year or severe self-harm is apparent, a doctor can categorise it as TS. The

[11] (n.d.). Tics & Tourette Syndrome - Movement Disorder Society. Retrieved May 7, 2020, from **https://www.movementdisorders.org/MDS/About/Movement-Disorder-Overviews/Tics--Tourette-Syndrome.htm**

[12] (n.d.). Coprolalia - Wikipedia. Retrieved May 8, 2020, from **https://en.wikipedia.org/wiki/Coprolalia**

[13] (n.d.). Tourette Syndrome Fact Sheet - NINDS - NIH. Retrieved May 7, 2020, from **https://www.ninds.nih.gov/Disorders/Patient-Caregiver-Education/Fact-Sheets/Tourette-Syndrome-Fact-Sheet**

tics, as mentioned earlier, are mostly due to external factors, and it is crucial to identify those environments. This way, we can fight the spasms and learn how to control them eventually. OCD and ADHD come hand in hand with Tics or Tourette's syndrome.[14]

When a teen already has conditions such as Tourette syndrome, OCD, and ADHD, it's challenging to tell which Behaviour is related to what condition. OCD and Tourette have similar feelings and compulsions. Bipolar is in my family Gene's, and I have a milder form of Bipolar called cyclothymic. So how are parents to know when Bipolar appears alongside the other conditions?

Two years after Ramani got diagnosed with Tourette, he started showing signs of reduced attention span, restlessness, hyperactivity. He was falling behind in his schoolwork. After the school called me in, I sat down with the teachers who were concerned about Ramani's Behaviour. I had to listen to what the teachers' fears were.

I had to remind them that he has Tourette's and OCD, which they acknowledged. They told me Ramani was unable to concentrate, unable to sit still, was very compulsive. They spoke of Behaviour, such as running in and out of the classroom. They asked if he had anything else diagnosed. No, there were no other diagnostics with new conditions, but it forced me to think, should he have more? Do the teachers see something I do not?

---

[14] (n.d.). Tourette Syndrome (for Kids) - Nemours KidsHealth. Retrieved May 7, 2020, from https://kidshealth.org/en/kids/k-tourette.html

After getting reviews from each tutor of Ramani, I realised how much he was struggling in school. I had to take him for an assessment with his paediatric neurologist, who had diagnosed his Tourette's. Ramani was also suffering from anxiety around the same time, where he felt nervous going out in public. Later, having the teachers filling in a tick-box questionnaire of around 50 questions, the specialist reviewed the outcome. Ramani was now also diagnosed with ADHD. Attention Deficit Hyperactivity Disorder. ADHD is known for hyperactivity and attention difficulties, which is another co-morbid condition with Tourette's syndrome.

Doesn't this child already have enough to handle? What is the next step for him? Moreover, how is he going to cope up in school any further?

In the doctor's office, where the first ADHD diagnosis took place, the neurologist also suggested a trial of medication for Ramani. I had no other option but to try him on medicine because he immensely struggled in school. We went through two different treatments for ADHD because the first medicine didn't work out well. However, luckily the second one he's on is making him able to manage more naturally. Although it will not solve the problems completely, it was enough to maintain him better than he was.

ADHD:

Attention deficit hyperactivity disorder (ADHD) is one of the most common mental health problems for youngsters. In the USA, for instance, a national-level survey concluded the number of children with ADHD is more than six million.[15] This figure is enormous!

---

[15] (2020, January 21). Attention deficit hyperactivity disorder (ADHD) - Statista. Retrieved May 7, 2020, from https://www.statista.com/topics/5079/attention-deficit-hyperactivity-disorder-adhd-in-the-us/

As the name suggests, the affected child will have a deficiency of attention and focus. Those children have problems performing better at school or socialising with their friends. Genetics is the primary cause, and head injury or premature deliveries come down in the list. The treatments involve training of parents, behavioural therapy for the kid, medication, or a combination of all. [16]

Ramani's anxiety started to become worse, and his fear became extreme and real to him. He believed people looking at him when passing by, are out to get him, to kill or kidnap him. This imagination has taken over his social life. However, he worked a lot with CBT (Cognitive behavioural therapy) to learn ways to change his thoughts and Behaviour to extreme fears. It is a talking therapy, where you talk a person out of a problematic situation.[17] With my education and training, I can help Ramani question him when he is feeling fearful and having wicked thoughts.

How could you treat these disorders? A doctor may suggest medicine. The side effects of the medication may be worse than the symptoms themselves. Nevertheless, if the tics get in the way of their daily lives, people can be treated with medicine. Therapy can teach coping and relaxation skills that can assist. Counsellors and Tourette syndrome organisations can help kids learn how to explain tics to others. Behavioural therapy may also aid. [18]

---

[16] (2020, April 8). What is ADHD? | CDC. Retrieved May 7, 2020, from https://www.cdc.gov/ncbddd/adhd/facts.html

[17] (n.d.). Cognitive behavioural therapy (CBT) - NHS. Retrieved May 7, 2020, from https://www.nhs.uk/conditions/cognitive-behavioural-therapy-cbt/

[18] (n.d.). Tics & Tourette Syndrome - Movement Disorder Society. Retrieved May 7, 2020, from https://www.movementdisorders.org/MDS/About/Movement-Disorder-Overviews/Tics--Tourette-Syndrome.htm

5th Chapter: Tics and the battle with the GP

One specialist tried accusing me of emotionally abusing my son Ramani because I was taking him to too many different doctors. What was I supposed to do when we were not getting a diagnosis?

It wasn't until I had my last referral to a London Tourette's specialist, who shed light on the chronic issue. The doctor questioned him about his tics and family background, which I had stated that his younger brother has now started to develop tics. This outcome was after an effort of eight years of fighting and trying to support my son. The doctor then asked to show him a video I had. Within 30 seconds into the video, he diagnosed my son with Tourette and OCD! The relief I felt, I did it, I won the fight, I knew it! Let's kick off with how I battled with the Medical Department.

It was Ramani who needed medical attention, and I had to take him to the GP, where they referred my son's case to the more resourceful facility. At the first child development appointment, they declared it only as a habit and that he will outgrow it! I felt ignored. A few months later, my son developed, alongside his eye-rolling tics, a mouth opening or what I'd call a mouth-pulling jerk of exasperation. Not long after showing OCD behaviour and hyperactivity, he started to develop another twitch licking his lips over and over again until they were red raw and cracked.

My other son, Rhys, had developed the ODD and hair-pulling condition called Trichotillomania, who had started with tics after my first child with Tourette. It was so much for me, and I had to fight at every stage of life. It took me eight years to get Ramani diagnosed with Tourette's. The consultants always told me that he would outgrow it. Doctors were in constant need of updates and more information regularly from me. This indication was visible for around six months on and off. Once more, the doctors and specialists told me it was a habit, and he outgrows this.

Now, after some more time, my son, Ramani, who already had Tics related to eyes and mouth, then developed a grunting sound from his throat. Grunting is a vocal tic I had researched, and to which I tried to stress to our newly referred specialists, they ignored us yet again!

I started to keep a diary of all current tics and new ones; also, new Behaviour and I video recorded his worst days. The school never noticed any twitches. Even when we were at the doctor's appointments, he never showed spasms. Why? I frazzled myself how could this be possible that no one sees his tics other than being at home with his father on weekends or with me! I stressed to numerous specialists and our family that this is what I believe it was, and they still discounted us.

After speaking to his teacher one day asking if he's seen any tics, the tutor told me that my son never showed any spasms in school and was told maybe he was jittery at home! Wow, now I'm to blame! The teacher thinks I'm lying! Later after some time, I asked his educator to watch a recording that I had of my son sitting calmly and relaxed on my sofa watching television. His teacher was shocked!

The instructor told me that my son looks calm and not worried and never seen any of this in his lessons.

I have kept many years of diaries that I had kept updated on my kids' Tics and OCD behaviour and other conditions that appeared alongside. My advice to anyone would first be to keep a diary. Logs of everything from new tics, to sleep patterns and other behaviours you believe aren't what you expect.

Furthermore, you should do your research first, as much as you can, join online groups, speak to others who have children with Tics and OCD, and get more facts on what Tourette is. Before you go to your consultant, take all your points, research diaries, and any recordings you have about your child. Without knowing the facts and the criteria for diagnosis, the specialists seldom try to mislead and ignore you. When you sit in front of specialists with the right info, then you have more chances they will listen to you and be obliged to go with your advice and knowledge.

I was no way quitting with the docs when I knew I was right. As a mother of four boys, I know my children more than anyone does. I had to get the correct diagnosis for my son to be able to move him forward with the right help and support, and I am glad I did. Because when he got to age 11 and started secondary school, that is when he needed help the most, and without the diagnosis, I fought for him. He would not have had the support and be where he is now.

Another good thing with my bipolar condition and me is once I'm stuck on an interest or subject, I can't stop; I get obsessed. I have an intense happy feeling in me when I am researching something in which I'm highly interested. Therefore, my condition is not all bad things for me because I stuck to this fight for eight years. Can you imagine?

My lowest point was when one consultant tried blaming me for Emotional Abuse. He negated me by saying, I was taking my son to too many docs and not accepting their outcome. I felt crisp and a bad mum when judged by a professional in such passion. It did not stop me, or nothing came out of it, but it was my darkest hour. I hit rock bottom that day, and I cried and broke down, only to get back up to fight again. It had made me want to prove her wrong and that I did. After an exact year, my son got the Tourette's diagnosis - I was telling her all along!

6th Chapter: The other Ticcsters

Now, my son Ramani was aged eight by then. Around this time, his younger brother Rhys, who is one year younger than he is, started to develop symptoms. The other two brothers began showing signs just before the diagnosis of Ramani's TS. Their traits were motor tics, excessive eye blinking, nose twitching, lip licking, and sniffing. Now, this is serious, and I want answers. I had to take Rhys & Rye for assessments too. We attended many appointments, and they only provided us with more referrals.

Only recently, in 2019, Doctors diagnosed Rhys with ODD, Oppositional Defiant Disorder. A condition that makes it challenging for Rhys to abide by the rules. As a result, he takes the word lightly. Rhys will refuse many instructions and become violent and rude. He also has social and emotional difficulties, meaning he can become easily upset for something minimal. His emotions are unstable and can change very quickly. Learning to manage this and support him, we went to therapy. We helped teach him ways to be able to cope with specific stresses and anxiety.

Maybe best I explain their ages: Rye is 19, Ramani 13 Rhys 12 and Kodie 6.

Rhys's Obsessive Compulsive Disorder was mainly a reassurance type. Having to ask questions, even though he knew the answer, but to him, he had the compulsion to ask to feel safe and to continue his task. Every time he would close the fridge door, then had to reopen the door and close to confirm it was shut. The same with car doors, he would have to open and close to reassure himself of the locked doors. This act was his OCD behaviour and was different to Ramani's.

During this time, when Rhys was showing signs of tics, my eldest son Rye had then started to have spasms. His twitches included a mouth opening movement, eyes roaming to one side. He later developed sniffing, and muscles were pulling on the neck! Rye had a similar OCD/paranoia to me, having to check the windows, hallways, and doors that no one was there because he felt he was at harm. This terror is Ramani's latest struggle with his paranoia when he is to walk outside alone. Now there's a genetic thing going on here, and it most definitely isn't from their dad because they have different fathers. Not only has my eldest now gotten tics, but also Dermatillomania, where he picks at his skin.

Dermatillomania:
It is a chronic skin-picking mental illness directly proportional to OCD (Obsessive Compulsive Disorder). When someone picks his/her skin repeatedly, without thinking of the pros and cons, it causes skin wounds. The lesions make the skin red, hurt, and result in tissue damage, but the person can't help with the constant pinch. One should try home remedies to avoid Dermatillomania as mentioned below, but if the urge is causing distress or damaging the skin severely, visiting the GP is suggested.

One can stop the "habit" by keeping their hands busy all the time. If your hands are free, you would unintentionally start biting them—the best way to go about holding a softball in your hand and squeezing it. Other natural ways include wearing gloves. You would need to establish the triggers for Dermatillomania, and avoid those. Applying petroleum jelly on the affected areas will stop you from picking your skin. Even your loved ones can help you avoid the situation, as they could prevent you as soon as you take your hands to mouth. It is best to resist the urge for the most extended periods, if possible.[19]

So many things are similar to me, and three boys of mine with their symptoms appearing gradually, I started worrying about their youngest brother. As for Kodie, he's only six, well passed Ramani's age of "patient zero." Ramani first showed the signs at the age of three. I had gone through all this experience, having to research everything from Tourette, OCD, ADHD, and Paranoia, then being aware of my mental health. I was in no doubt that I'd be able to see early signs in my youngest if there were any. Now I have noticed his tics, and I'm going through it all once again.

It was a lot for me to go through the diagnosis for Ramani and then the continuance of support to my other two, showing challenging Behaviour. Ramani started year seven secondary school, and by Easter that year, he was becoming difficult. Poor attention, restlessness, tics becoming more apparent, impulsive ways, and more. After some more assessments, they diagnosed my son with ADHD and put him on medication.

Later on, Rhys had visible OCD manners. This way of behaving meant having to do routines and equal things out to feel right. When I got his Behaviour evaluated by therapists, they diagnosed him with

[19] (n.d.). Skin picking disorder - NHS. Retrieved May 6, 2020, from https://www.nhs.uk/conditions/skin-picking-disorder/

OCD. The therapists also diagnosed him with Trichotillomania. It is a condition where the person pulls his hair out.

Further assessments detected the ODD oppositional defiant disorder in Rhys. Now, as a family, we had ample things going on. It seems there's a powerful connection from my Gene's and the neurological resemblance. I have Bipolar disorder, BPD, tics, and OCD. Ramani, at age 12, was then diagnosed with paranoia and possibly Bipolar!

Since we're suffering from conditions a lot more than Tics Disorders, it is imperative to define those terms/conditions here for your better understanding.

ODD:
The oppositional defiant disorder is a youngster's continuous pattern of being rebellious, angry, arrogant, or spiteful against the elders, even his parents. It is the severe mood swings of a child. Your paediatrician or the mental health expert can assist you in overcoming this disorder, and you do not have to do it alone.

You can develop learning skills in the child to control his Behaviour and to be polite. Improving positivity in the minds of children seems the only possible solution for the treatment of ODD.[20]

The experts told us to keep a diary of any odd conduct than usual. On big days, he won't sleep or eat, gets goofy, acts drunk, and needs

[20] (n.d.). Oppositional Defiant Disorder (ODD) in Children | Johns .... Retrieved May 7, 2020, from **https://www.hopkinsmedicine.org/health/conditions-and-diseases/oppositional-defiant-disorder**

a lot of my attention. When he has a low mood, he will not wake up, feel exhausted, and can't do anything. Other days when he feels hyper and down altogether, he suddenly becomes tired after being active and goes to sleep. This episode was only to wake up one hour later, becoming active all over again.

I also have my youngest boy Kodie. He is six years old. I believed for the past two years that Kodie has no signs of tics or behavioural problems. Aged 4 Kodie still has no symptoms, and I'm happy because undoubtedly one of my kids needs to be free from difficulties! Kodie shows signs now aged 6 of dyslexia, but still, early days to test, so they told me. Anyway, I was recording Kodie singing a song and looked closely at him, and guess what? He has a lip-licking and lip-biting tic. Oh, my God! I am now just shaken and scared of what the future is for him now. His mouth was all red raw and sore. How can this happen? Not my little boy!

As a parent and knowing the genetic connections already with Ramani, Rhys, and Rye has tics, and other comportments, Kodie showing these new twitches with lip-licking is worrying. For what am I to expect next? Is he going to have a shrugging spasm appearing or swearing tics, is he going to develop OCD manners the same as the other three boys and myself?

7th Chapter: What you allow will continue!

It was about two years before Ramani got diagnosed with the TS that Rhys showed eye squinting tics, mouth-licking, and nose scrunching. Moreover, Rhys had a vocal tic for a few months of a clicking sound at the back of his throat. Not long after, I noticed Rye was showing neck muscle tensing, sniffing, eye-rolling upwards, and mouth opening. I didn't understand that Tourette's are genetic, yet. When I would tell the docs about Ramani and the other two boys are now showing Tics, every doctor ignored me for so long.

At this time, Rye was picking the skin of his hands around his thumbs excessively to make them bleed and red. After having to attend doctors for him and mention his spasms and skin picking, they diagnosed him with tic disorder and Dermatillomania. Additionally, he suffered from OCD. Around the same year, I had to see a separate doctor for Rhys regarding his tics and OCD, as he developed a hair-pulling condition called Trichotillomania. When anxious or nervous, Rhys would pull his hair on his head to feel relaxed and relieved.

Trichotillomania

You can read it out like Trico-Tillo-Mania. It is also under the umbrella of OCD and is a subsequent disorder. Trichotillomania is a disorder where a person starts pulling hair from the scalp. It could also be related to other body parts with hair, like eyebrows and eyelids. It might result in the removal of hair and succeed by hair loss.

This hair-pulling disorder can play as an occupational hazard for the person affected. One can become socially distressed, as you would only feel relieved after pulling the hair. Anxiety triggers Trichotillomania, so it is crucial to stay calm and avoid those nervous moments. If you think the disorder is creating functional problems in your life, you must visit your doctor and seek his guidance. [21]

Most of these conditions are neurological disorders and are a stable link with my Gene's. They have different dads; clearly, it's from me where the Genes are. It is a lot for me to take in, and I always consider that their problems are from me.

Rhys was only diagnosed last year with ODD. Therefore, I am still in the stage of getting support for him in school. Kodie, my youngest, only started showing those mouth-licking tics previous year too, and I didn't notice how badly until I recorded him singing. I mentioned it to his dad, whom I separated from 5 years ago. Even though his biological father knew about Ramani and his other son Rhys with tics, he denied. My youngest son Kodie is having spasms, and the guy says its a habit! Strange how he can assume that knowing his genetic links with us all. Maybe he doesn't want to see his 2nd son having spasms, but denying that will not solve the problem, supporting will.

---

[21] (2018, February 13). What is Trichotillomania? A Closer Look at Hair ... - Psycom. Retrieved May 6, 2020, from **https://www.psycom.net/what-is-trichotillomania/**

CBT therapy taught both of us to change our ways of thinking. I'd use this technique whenever Ramani would tell me, when we were in the local store, that someone is watching me. I would then question his belief by asking him, 'what proof do you have that someone is watching you" how about that person is looking at something or someone else next to you"? He would reply, but the man is following me. I'd then again question this thought by asking him, "What are the chances the man only wants to buy something in the same aisle as you and isn't intended to follow you? What makes you believe this person has an interest in just you, and how often has someone ever come behind you to harm you? His response, after much thinking, would now become a more positive thought. This technique usually works.

Furthermore, I taught him this: What you allow will continue!

At present, we are doing the best we can in the given circumstances. My training aids me to develop a positive mindset in the kids. The more recent concern for me, as a mother, is that Ramani has developed new symptoms. The poor soul has new expressions of ADHD and Paranoia, and he is currently monitored for Bipolar. Since his genes come from me, I often blame myself. Is it OK to feel me as the reason for my children's conditions? Did I contribute my two-cents to the spreading awareness of Tourette's?

Although I had experienced a plethora of negative things growing up, I can say that I have learnt so much in all this time. Moreover, I went through the struggles in my own family life with my kids' health. I have developed a lot of knowledge of mental health conditions and relationships. I learnt CBT therapy, studied courses, and much more.

I have also managed to gain a happier and stable family life and, most importantly, self-respect. I cannot change my past because that's the reason I am who I am now.
I am ending the book here, not my story!

MY STORY ISN'T OVER

The Four Ticcsters

Family of Tics, Tourette's & More

Caris Poynter

Printed in Great Britain
by Amazon

81180210R00027